SERMON OUTLINES
on

Coming to Christ

Charles R. Wood

PUBLICATIONS

Grand Rapids, MI 49501

Sermon Outlines on Coming to Christ

© 1991 by Charles R. Wood

Published by Kregel Publications, a division of Kregel, Inc., P.O. Box 2607, Grand Rapids, MI 49501. Kregel Publications provides trusted, biblical publications for Christian growth and service. Your comments and suggestions are valued.

For more information about Kregel Publications, visit our web site at: www.kregel.com

Cover design: Frank Gutbrod

Library of Congress Cataloging-in-Publication
Sermon outlines on coming to Christ / by Charles R. Wood.
       p.   cm.
1. Regeneration (Theology)—Sermons—Outlines, syllabi, etc.
I. Title. II. Charles R. Wood.
BT790.W78   1991   91-27155
252'.02—dc20

ISBN 0-8254-4127-7

2 3 4 5 / 04 03

Printed in the United States of America

Contents

Textual Index

Introduction

At a time when the influence of Christianity appears to be at an all time low, claims of being "born again" appear to have reached an all time high. It is common for politicians, athletes, business executives, show business personalities, rock musicians, and just about anyone else who feels like it to claim "born again status." The visible end results in many cases, however, leave one wondering if what is claimed bears any real relationship to what the Bible presents.

Clearly the time has come for a re-examination of biblical teaching regarding what is involved in and required for the new birth. The recorded New Testament instances in which people came to Christ and found new life in Him present a picture of change and renewal that contrasts vividly with the results of the currently popular "make a decision for Christ" that characterizes so much evangelism.

The sermon outlines in this book seek to view the new birth from a biblical standpoint, to examine anew its actual meaning, and to treat its claims with a sacred seriousness. In the process, messages that touch on related topics, such as salvation, spiritual renewal, Christian growth, etc., are included to give a broad-based treatment to the subject. Salvation is treated as involving something more than human relationship, a growing process of belief, verbal assent to a presentation, or simple response to an "invitation" at a meeting.

The Bible clearly teaches that the new birth involves a recognition of sin and a desire to turn from it along with an internal change wrought within the individual by the work of the Holy Spirit. These messages are designed to enable the preacher to win men to Christ rather than merely to bring them to the point of making a decision.

The messages were prepared and preached by the editor. They are based on careful exegesis of the passages, an attention to proper canons of biblical interpretation, and thoughtful examination of relevant literature to determine the correctness of the positions taken. At the time they were preached, several of these messages resulted in people coming to trust Christ as personal Savior. Thus they have not only been "tried," but they have also been proven capable of accomplishing their stated purpose.

These sermons are not designed for presentation without preparation. They are rather ideally suited for the busy pastor who needs "seed thoughts" or finds himself short of adequate time to allow for original preparation. They will assist in the study of the passage and in the presentation of the results of that study. No one should hesitate to alter any outline to accommodate the findings of his own investigation. They are designed to be preached, not parroted.

In an age when many are decrying the lack of interest in spiritual things shown by society in general, personal experience has demonstrated that there are many who will come to Christ if the presentation of biblical truth is clear, logical and sincerely expressed. It is the prayer of the editor that God may use these messages on the lips of prepared messengers to bring many to a saving knowledge of Jesus Christ.

May we all have a renewed understanding of the gravity of Christ's words when He said, "Except a man be born again, he cannot see the kingdom of God."

The Wages of Sin
Genesis 3:1-19

Introduction:
   If you do it, it's a personality quirk, a habit, or just a "little thing."
If someone else does it, it's disgusting, unnecessary, foolish, annoy-
ing, or sinful. We surely have built up defense mechanisms around
our own conduct. This can be deadly!

I. **The Sickness**
   A. It all began in the Garden of Eden
      1. This is a literal historical account
      2. It traces the beginning of sin
      3. Everyone living now would have done the same thing
   B. It brought enormous changes to man
      1. His make-up
      2. His location
      3. His relationships
      4. His situation
      5. His destiny

II. **The Symptoms**
   A. Blame shifting
      1. "The woman . . . The man" (12-13)
      2. Each was quick to blame the other
   B. Self seeking
      1. ". . . desired to make one wise . . ." (6)
      2. We continually look out for number one
   C. Pride
      1. "Ye shall be as God . . ." (4)
      2. Our tendency is to elevate ourselves
   D. Desire/feeling orientation
      1. ". . . Pleasant to the eyes . . . Desired" (6)
      2. Most of our lives are lived on the basis of feeling.
   E. Rebellion
      1. "She took and did eat . . . and he did eat" (6)
      2. Every time we refuse to accept the teaching or direction
         of the Word of God, we are guilty of the same sin.
   F. Guilt
      1. The whole story is filled with this
      2. This was the result of unconfessed sin
   G. Fear
      1. "I was afraid" (10)
      2. Fear arises from broken communication with God
   H. Lying

1. "... I was naked." This was not the real reason
2. Lying is so common, but it does not have gradations
I. Breakdown of communication
   1. "Adam and his wife hid themselves"
   2. Sin is involved in every communication breakdown
J. Self-pity
   1. "Neither shall ye touch it"
   2. All self-pity is a sinful response

III. The Seriousness
A. Each symptom was part of the original sinful act
   1. They are all clearly revealed as sinful
   2. Each involves some clear violation of the Word of God
B. We regularly do these things
   1. They become part of our lives
   2. They are passed off, excused, or unrecognized
   3. If they are allowed long enough, they become habitual
C. All of these things lead on to some measure of misery
   1. They are ways in which we handle our problems
   2. They intensify and add to our problems
   3. They drive other people away from us
D. Each is sin and displeases God
   1. Every sin breaks fellowship with God
   2. Broken fellowship makes problems worse

IV. The Solution
A. We must agree with God
   1. We must call sin, sin
   2. We must admit that our conduct is improper
   3. We must admit that improper conduct is sin
B. We must desire change
   1. This involves a heart intention
   2. It may lead to some pain
   3. It involves willingness to work
C. We must apply the help at hand
   1. We must turn to the Word of God
   2. We must do what the Word says
   3. We must ask God to show us ourselves in the Word
D. We must call upon God for help
   1. This involves earnest prayer and proper practice
   2. Christ is the only real answer for sin

Conclusion:
"The heart is deceitful above all things and desperately wicked." How clearly this truth is shown here. The wages of sin is a mess and more trouble. The only answer is to recognize sin and turn to Christ for forgiveness and help or for salvation.

Confess Your Sins
Proverbs 28:13; 1 John 1:9

Introduction:
1 John 1:9 may be the greatest promise of the Word. It promises forgiveness for sin and cleansing for unrighteousness, but it is all conditioned by confession.

I.   **The Content of Confession (shown by David in Psalms 32:1-5 & 51:1-5)**
   A.   There must be an acknowledgment of basic sinfulness
      1.   We must recognize this exists
      2.   We do not have to confess this
   B.   There must be an admission of having done wrong
      1.   The "apology" was invented by the Devil to prevent confession
      2.   Admission must be to the one(s) wronged
   C.   There must be an agreement with God that what has been done is sin
      1.   This is the real meaning of confession
      2.   This is a basic need, and there is no relief without it
   D.   There must be an assessment of effects
      1.   It is important to identify them
      2.   All sin is against God, but others are involved as well (Cf. Psalm 51:4)

II. **The Constraints of Confession**
   A.   Blameshifting
   B.   Excuses
   C.   Pride
   D.   Personal definitions of sin
   E.   Confession with lips only (getting God or others off my back)
   E.   Rationalization
   F.   Apology

III. **The Cautions of Confession**
   A.   There is no efficacy in corporate confession
      1.   It is done in the Bible but in a different context
      2.   It is done in many churches
   B.   There is no biblical grounds for "auricular" confession
      1.   It is a Catholic church practice
      2.   Confession to man may be helpful
      3.   Man certainly can't forgive, so such confession is neither called for nor required

C. There is no warrant for a confession more general than the extent to which the sin is known
   1. There are sins of heart, and there are sins of social consequences
   2. Heart sins are confessed to God
   3. Social consequence sins are confessed to the people involved
   4. Public knowledge is the important criteria
D. No morbid self-introspection is called for
E. No general catch-all phrases are useful

Conclusion:

The real concern of genuine confession is with the one who has been wronged. Confession never stands alone; it is always accompanied by at least a desire for change. Confession and repentance go together. Have you confessed your sin? Have you some unconfessed sins?

Full Forgiveness, Can It Be?

Jeremiah 31:34

Introduction:

If God would meet only one need of man, what need should be met? I would suggest forgiveness, for without that need met nothing else matters. God has already met that need.

I. **The Need of Forgiveness**
   A. The need is created by man's guilt
   B. Guilt comes in two forms
      1. Psychology speaks of real and false guilt
      2. Actually, all guilt is real; the question is whether it is deserved or undeserved
   C. Deserved guilt is caused by violations of the divine law

II. **The Nature of Forgiveness**
   A. There are various usages of the word
      1. Let go (Matthew 4:30)
      2. Send away from oneself (Matthew 13:36)
      3. Turn away from (Matthew 19:29)
      4. Pass over (Matthew 23:23)
   B. It is not a feeling
   C. A dual promise—(Jeremiah 31:34)
      1. To lift the burden of guilt
      2. To remember wrong no more
      a. Not to you
      b. Not to others
      c. Not to myself
   D. Forgiveness: "Lifting of guilt from another, and a promise that it will not be remembered again in the future."

III. **The Norm of Forgiveness**
   A. The teaching of Christ (Luke 17:3)
      1. Go to one who has wronged you and rebuke him
      2. Forgive
      a. If he repents
      b. As often as he repents
      c. On the basis of His Word alone
      d. Whether or not you feel like it
      e. Because God commands it
   B. Note: He would not expect us to do what He would not do

IV. **The Neglect of Forgiveness (Matthew 6:8-15)**

A. Must we forgive to be forgiven?
   1. There is much misinterpretation of this passage
      a. This is not earned righteousness
      b. It is a sign of being forgiven
   2. He is speaking here of a different kind of forgiveness
      a. It is not judicial as that is covered by Christ
      b. It is parental (note "father" uses)
   3. As God's children we cannot expect forgiveness of our sins if we refuse to forgive others
B. Must we forgive and forget?
   1. We must forgive in order to forget
   2. When we really forgive, forgetting will come as a result

V. The Necessities of Forgiveness

A. We must forgive from our hearts in every instance (Mark 11:25)
B. We must grant forgiveness whenever it is requested (Matthew 18:31-35)
C. There must be repentance and confession in order for there to be granted forgiveness
   1. Repentance and confession are necessary for our SIN to be forgiven
   2. Repentance and confession are necessary for our SINS to be forgiven
   3. Repentance and confession are necessary for our wrong toward others to be forgiven (that's why an "apology" is pointless)

Conclusion:

There is no greater burden than the burden of guilt for sin. There is no other way to have it really lifted than through forgiveness. There is no other path to forgiveness than confession. God can forgive anything you have ever done. God can forgive all you have ever done. What is needed is repentance.

For He Shall Save His People From Their Sins
Matthew 1:18-25

Introduction:

The words, "Good tidings of great joy to all people," sound like a mockery, but they are true. This passage probably does more to demonstrate that truth than any in the Bible. Note the phrase, "For He shall save His people from their sins," which becomes the heart of our message.

I. **The Problem**
   A. Sin is the problem man faces
   B. Note the two levels of man's sinfulness: sin and sins
   C. Doing something about sins implies doing something about sin, because sins arise from sin

II. **The Provision**
   A. Sin is the problem; "shall save" is the provision
   B. What sin does to man
      1. It dominates him
      2. It destroys him
      3. It damns him
   C. Christ came "to save" people from all of that

III. **The Provider**
   A. "He"—refers to Christ
   B. He is the One who can do something about sin
   C. Notice that He is the only One that can do anything about sin

IV. **The Participants**
   A. It is limited to "His people"
   B. It refers to relationship
   C. The only way to find the provision is through relationship

Conclusion:

There is joy at Christmas and at all other times because God has done something about the sin of mankind. Have you found His provision? Are you claiming His provision?

Reach Out

Introduction:

Most Christians are glad they are believers. Most would really like to see others become Christians. Most believe they are responsible to work to that end. Most, however, don't do very much about it. It may be that a new look at outreach might be helpful.

I. **The Statement of Our Problem**
   A. There are many approaches to winning the lost, and each seems to have its problems
      1. It is better to do something than nothing
      2. It is better still to sharpen what one does to make it more effective
   B. There are many violations of the New Testament pattern (Acts 2:41-47)
      1. The New Testament pattern: saved, baptized, added to church, begin to participate, win others
      2. Very few go on to win others
   C. Some practical problems
      1. Statistics become an end in themselves
      2. We work on the law of averages
      3. We give false assurance by having people "pray a prayer"
      4. Many are turned off by such approaches
   D. If a person genuinely trusts Christ, he is saved whether or not he is baptized, attends church, etc., but it is much like getting married and then separating

II. **The Portrait of Our Problem**
   A. A familiar story here
      1. The parable is designed to teach one main truth
      2. The whole chapter teaches that truth: the way things are supposed to be at the present, and the way they actually are
   B. It does show:
      1. The problem is not the sower or the seed but the place where the seed landed
      2. The kind of ground determined the results rather than the sower or the seed
      3. The basic teaching is not which ones were saved but rather, "you can't win them all"
      4. The real emphasis here is on following through and bearing fruit

14

C. It tells us something we need to know about our problems
1. Not everyone reached produces
2. There are many reasons for blocked fruit
3. Our job is to sow; then it is God's job to produce the harvest
4. We must be careful of what we sow, as bad seed produces no fruit

III. The Solution to Our Problem
A. A recognition
1. There are many conversion stories in the Word
2. They are almost all different. There is no set formula
B. The irreducible minimum
1. What is the least one can believe and be saved?
2. Likely much less than most of us think!
C. The absolute essential
1. Not what some evangelist or preacher says
2. Repentance—a willingness and desire for change

Conclusion:
We need some method. We may not have the best or most biblical, because that method is much more difficult. It involves all of life. True "lifestyle evangelism" is the best method.

The Way He Works
Mark 2:1-12

Introduction:

Christ had been away from Capernaum for a while. He returns, and the welcome creates a mob. A man is totally paralyzed and dependent. His friends bring him to Jesus, but they can't get in. Someone gets the idea of entry through the roof. In response to the situation, Jesus heals the man and forgives his sins. In the process, Christ shows how He works when He heals men of their sins and forgives them.

I. **He Deals With a Man Incapable**
   A. He was totally dependent on others even to get to Christ
   B. Jesus always comes to men who are incapable
      1. Men who are capable do not need Him (cf. vs. 16 & 17)
      2. Total depravity here—not that we are as bad as we could be, but that we can do nothing in ourselves to please God

II. **He Calls Upon Him to Do What He Cannot Do**
   A. Christ calls upon him to arise. If he could do so, he wouldn't be where he is
   B. Christ calls upon men to do what they cannot do, to trust Him as Lord and Savior
      1. No man, unaided by the Holy Spirit, can do so
      2. Salvation is thus a theoretical impossiblity

III. **He Enables Him to Do What He Cannot Do**
   A. As soon as He issues the command, the man does it
   B. When Christ calls upon a sinner to believe, he cannot do it, but the moment he begins to do it he is able to do it

IV. **He Is Healed Immediately**
   A. The man's paralysis would make one think that it would be a process of healing. Instead, it is absolutely immediate
   B. Salvation is immediate and complete. It is not something to be grown into
      1. When we are saved, we are saved at once
      2. When we are saved, we are saved completely

V. **He Is Healed Without Any Ceremony**
   A. Christ dispensed with normal procedures and healed in the simplest manner possible
   B. Salvation is devoid of any procedures
      1. There is no ceremony necessary

2. There is nothing that any ceremony can add to the completeness of salvation

VI. He Is Healed Perfectly
A. There was nothing lacking in his new condition
B. Salvation is perfect. Christ provides all we need for time and eternity

VII. He Is Healed Obviously
A. Christ handled the healing in such a way that it was plain for all to see what had happened
B. Salvation, when it is genuine, will also be plain for all to see.
1. When salvation makes no changes, it raises questions about its real genuineness
2. If there is nothing in your life that is different or obvious, it ought to make you wonder whether or not something has happened

Conclusion:
Have you ever had the fantastic experience this man had? Have you trusted Him and found Him complete and perfect to meet your needs? Is anything happening in your life which demonstrates clearly that something has taken place?

The Reasons Why

Mark 10:17-22

Introduction:

It is easy for Christians to say, "I can't see why everyone isn't a Christian." But there are reasons why men don't come to Christ, and they are usually different from the reasons given. Four of the main reasons men don't come to Christ are illustrated by the man in this story.

I. **He Failed to Understand Who Christ Was—"Good Master"**
   A. Note the attitude of his approach
      1. He was respectful ("Good Master")
      2. He was sincere (note his whole demeanor)
      3. He was genuinely seeking (he came running)
      4. He regarded Christ highly (he kneeled down)
   B. Christ's answer pointed up his problem
      1. "Why callest me Good? There is none good but one—God"
      2. If Christ is good then He is God; if He is not God, He is not good
   C. The problem keeps men from Christ
      1. Men must do something to explain Christ
      2. Christ must be what He claimed to be, or He is unworthy of attention

II. **He Failed to Understand Spiritual Things—"What shall I do that I may inherit eternal life?"**
   A. Note the question
      1. What "good thing" (Matthew 19:17)? He was seeking something tangible
      2. "Must I do?" He was involved in his own effort
      3. "To inherit eternal life?"
   B. Note Christ's unusual answer
      1. He quotes the second table of the law
      2. This was the only possible answer to the question that he asked
      3. Christ used the second table for a reason. Love for man is easy compared to love for God
      4. Christ also said, "Come, follow me"
   C. This problem keeps men from Christ. What must I DO?
      1. There is no other answer than what Christ gave
      2. The only thing you can DO to inherit eternal life is perfectly keep the law

III. **He Failed to Understand Himself—"All these have I observed from my youth"**
  A. He was probably sincere
  B. Christ doesn't comment on whether or not he was right
     1. Christ simply suggests he sell all he has
     2. Christ is showing him that his unwillingness to do so gives the lie to his boast of having kept the law
  C. This problem keeps men from Christ
     1. Men don't come to Christ because they don't feel they are bad enough
     2. Men don't come to Christ because they think they have done everything required

IV. **He Failed to Understand Proper Priorities—"He . . . went away grieved; for he had great possessions"**
  A. He came with interest and sincerity; he goes away without a word because of the nature of the demand
  B. Christ comments on his departure (23-27)
     1. The real problem was materialism
     2. Materialism is an attitude
     3. Materialism does negative things to us
  C. This problem keeps men from Christ
     1. Many fail to see their need because they "have" so much
     2. Others have their vision obscured
     3. Still others won't come to Him for fear of losing something
     4. Materialism can keep sinners from Christ and saints from blessing equally well

Conclusion:
There are good reasons why men don't come to Christ. Some of them are:
  1. They don't understand Who He is.
  2. They misunderstand the spiritual and think they can earn an inheritance.
  3. They don't know themselves well enough to know their own need.
  4. They are too taken with the material and earthly.

What is keeping you from coming to Christ?

Too Bad and Not Good Enough

Mark 10:17-22; 12:28-34

Introduction:

Interview one hundred people on the street at random and ask them how one may get to heaven. Ninety-five percent will give one of two answers: 1) You have to do enough good. 2) You have to avoid doing bad. Salvation is usually seen as a matter of goodness, good works, avoidance of evil, etc. Exactly the same situation pertained in the days of Christ, and He addressed it squarely.

I. Christ and the Law (Mark 12:28-34)
    A. The Ten Commandments are a negative expression ("Thou shalt not . . .")
    B. They are also positive
        1. The "two great commandments" are a summary of the two tables of the law
        2. The correct application of them is both negative and completely positive
    C. They cover the ways in which most people believe salvation is found
        1. Either way, you are dealing with the Ten Commandments
        2. Something more is necessary to keep them than merely refraining from doing what they condemn

II. The Application of the Law (Mark 10:17-22)
    A. "What shall I do to inherit eternal life?"
        1. There is an inherent inaccuracy here, one normally does not "do" to inherit
        2. Christ ignores this and answers, "You know the commandments; keep them"
        3. It appears He is saying that salvation comes by this means
    B. "All these have I observed from my youth"
    C. Christ turns the Ten Commandments positive: "Go and sell what you have and give to the poor"
        1. This deals with the second Commandment, "thou shalt love thy neighbor"
        2. His unwillingness to do so shows that he does not keep the law. He is not good enough even though he does not violate the commandments

III. The Basic Issue of the Law
    A. Jesus said, "There is none good save God"
        1. He clearly points out that there is no man who is really good

2. If there is no man good, then there is no man who can do good
3. If God is good, no man can get to Him
B. Truth: there is no man who is good, and there is no good man can do, positively or negatively, that will qualify him with God
C. If man is going to satisfy God, the goodness must come from some other source
D. God has provided the good, Christ (2 Corinthians 5:21). He is good; He has died to make us good

Conclusion:

Most people expect to go to heaven by some form of goodness or absence of badness. This absolutely will not work. There is no possibility of good in man sufficient to satisfy God. Only the righteousness of Christ will work. You can't earn heaven by works in any form, you can only get it through accepting it from Christ.

The Meaning of Repentance

Luke 5:11-24

Introduction:

Two questions are frequently heard. Is repentance necessary to salvation? Can a man be restored to leadership after a failure? They may seem unrelated, but they actually go hand in hand.

I. **The Meaning of Repentance**
   A. Usually: sorrow for sin
   B. Biblically:
      1. A simple change of mind—especially as regards sin
      2. It involves
         a. Recognition and regret for past sin
         b. Desire and effort for change
      3. It is shown in life by fruit (evidence)

II. **The Demonstration of Repentance**
   A. He realized his desperate condition—"He came to himself"
   B. He made a mental determination to change his course— "I will arise and go to my father"
   C. He made a decisive act—breaking away and going back— "He arose and came to his father"
   D. He came with absolute humility—"I am unworthy"
   E. He openly, unreservedly, unqualifiedly confessed his sin— "I have sinned to the very heaven. . . ."

III. **The Issue in Repentance**
   A. Is repentance required for salvation?
      1. This is the wrong question. It should be, "Is repentance part of salvation?"
      2. These are two sides of the same coin
      3. It is difficult to conceive of salvation without some recognition of sin
   B. Can a leader who has fallen be restored to a position of leadership?
      1. This is the wrong question. The right one is, "Has the fallen leader shown any genuine evidence of repentance?"
      2. Restoration without repentance will issue in repeated offenses
      3. We can't discuss restoration until the issue of repentance is settled

Conclusion:

Without repentance—like the prodigal—there can be no restoration or reconciliation. Do you need to repent? Have you repented?

Except Ye Repent

Luke 13:1-5

Introduction:

Calamities are commonplace. Two had happened in recent times in Scripture. Pilate had killed some people who were offering sacrifices. A tower in Siloam had fallen and killed eighteen. Some were drawing wrong conclusions from these events. Jesus used the situation as an opportunity to correct their thinking and to teach eternal truth.

I. **A Correction: Calamity Is Proof of Nothing**
    A. Because we don't know what God is doing
        1. It may be chastisement
        2. It may be something unrelated
        3. It may be a time of testing
    B. Because we don't know how it will finally come out
    C. Because such thinking claims to understand the ways of God which are above finding out
    D. Because it assigns to the time of probation the ministry of judgment and punishment
        1. This day is the day of probation
        2. The future is the time of punishment
    E. Because it tends to take the focus off ourselves
        1. No doubt that these were Pharisees
        2. The fact that we have survived or do well is no proof of anything

II. **A Condition: "We Shall All Likewise Perish"**
    A. We are all destined to perish
        1. It is the price of sin—Romans 6:23
        2. It is common to all men—Hebrews 9:27
        3. It is eternal
        4. It is absolutely certain
    B. It is this that makes sense out of life now
        1. Things are not equitable
        2. The balances will be worked out

III. **A Correction: The Exception to Perishing Is Repentance**
    A. Repentance has a twofold meaning.
        1. To sense the nature of sin (the holiness of God and the awfulness of sin) produces sorrow
        2. To turn, or to be willing to turn, from sin
    B. Is repentance necessary to salvation?
        1. Repentance is part of the Gospel

2. Repentance is not some special thing we do to earn God's grace, but a part of the process of being saved
3. The problem with many "conversions" that don't appear genuine probably lies right here: there is no concept of sin and the need to turn from it
C. This is where all other approaches to salvation falter. There is no other way to avoid perishing than by turning from sin to the Savior
D. There is a note of warning to Christians here
1. There is a sense in which the Christian will perish unless he repents of cherished sin that is being cultivated
2. Whatever you have been clinging to that has been dishonoring the Lord and harming your spiritual life, deal with it before it deals with you

Conclusion:

This is a crucial passage. Repentance is necessary for salvation. But, repentance is not something separate, it is a part of conversion. Have you repented of your sin? Child of God, do you need some repentance?

Born Once: Born Twice
John 3:1-18

Introduction:

"Born again" is one of the hot terms of our times. The media criticizes it. Athletes, movie stars, and especially politicians all claim it. It is a good and valid term, but we need to be sure it is defined properly. It is easier to understand "born again" when we draw five likenesses between it and being born physically.

I. **Both Begin at a Point of Time**
   A. The point is not necessarily known, but there is one
      1. Some don't know for sure when they were born, but they are sure they were born at a point in time
      2. You may not know when you were born again as to day or date, but you must be sure you were
   B. This likeness rules out two common fallacies
      1. "I have always been a Christian"
      2. "I do that all the time"

II. **Both Involve a Change of Status**
   A. When you were born, some things changed; you were different from what you had been
   B. This becomes a significant point in the new birth
      1. When there are no changes, it raises the question of whether or not there has been a birth at all
      2. Not all changes come instantly, but there are significant changes
   C. If there are no changes, it surely raises the question of whether or not something has taken place

III. **Both Begin Periods of Growth**
   A. Natural birth results in growth or there is clear evidence of something wrong
      1. Growth tapers off after a while
      2. Lack of growth becomes a source of great concern
   B. Spiritual birth should begin a period of growth
      1. That growth never stops
      2. When there is no spiritual growth, there is a clear indication that something is wrong

IV. **Both Begin Something That Never Ends**
   A. The likeness is deliberate
      1. If human birth can end, and it never does, then spiritual birth can end
      2. No man can be unborn in either realm

25

B. There is much confusion in this area because men have tried to do the Lord's work for Him and to figure out ways to keep people from going into sin

V. Both Are Required for There to Be Meaningful Life
A. The child is alive before birth
   1. This is what makes abortion murder
   2. But meaningful life comes with birth
B. There is no meaningful spiritual life until the new birth
   1. No matter how good, religious, etc., a person may be, he has no life without the new birth
   2. Without the new birth, there is no eternal life either

Conclusion:

You must be straight on the matter of the new birth. Are you genuinely born again as the Bible teaches? You must make sure.

Born-Again But Not Saved

John 3:3

Introduction:

Over 50 percent of American adults profess to be "born-again." This sounds great, but there appears to be little evidence that it is true. Could it be that "born-again" has so changed in meaning that those professing it don't know what it really means? Matthew 7:21 clearly teaches this truth. There are many people today who profess to be born-again who are not saved. There are at least six groups.

I.   Those Who Have Been Baptized
   A.   Either as adults or infants, but trusting baptism for salvation
   B.   New Testament baptism doesn't save anyone

II. Those Who Have Spoken in Tongues
   A.   Nowhere does the Bible say that tongues prove salvation
      1.   Not everyone spoke in tongues (1 Corinthians 12:19-31)
      2.   A changed life is the biblical proof of salvation (Matthew 7:15-20)
   B.   Speaking in tongues does not prove one is born again.

III. Those Who Have Had a "Spiritual Experience"
   A.   Spiritual experiences are meaningless in regard to salvation
   B.   Trusting a spiritual experience will not save you from Hell

IV. Those Who Have Had a Moral Turn Around
   A.   Some people have moral turn arounds without religion (the strong willed and the very frightened)
   B.   If it is something you did, it couldn't save you

V.   Those Who Have Joined a Church
   A.   We believe in church membership
   B.   But no church saves, and the one that claims to is furthest away from the truth
   C.   Church membership will not avail at the Judgment

VI. Those Who Have Prayed a Prayer
   A.   Biblical salvation comes through a prayer requesting it
      1.   One can't be saved without accepting salvation
      2.   But one can pray a prayer and not mean it
   B.   A double caution is involved:
      1.   To those who seek to win the lost
      2.   To those who have merely prayed a prayer

Conclusion:

The only way to be saved is to admit one's sin, seek forgiveness, and accept what Christ has done. Have you done this? This is what it means to be "born-again."

Everyone's Favorite Bible Verse

John 3:1-21

Introduction:

John 3:16 is almost everyone's favorite verse. It is one of the most familiar in the Bible. Its popularity tends to obscure the important passage in which it occurs.

I. **The Occasion of the Teaching (1 & 2)**
   A. The coming of Nicodemus
      1. A religious man—a Pharisee and member of the Sanhedrin
      2. He was timid ("by night"), but he was an honest seeker
   B. His statement
      1. "Rabbi" was a term of respect
      2. He saw something special in Christ
      3. He saw Christ as just another teacher, and he was swayed by outward things

II. **The Essence of the Teaching (3-8)**
   A. Christ's statement, "except a man be born . . ."
      1. No question was asked that demanded this answer
      2. Nicodemus had Jewish expectations and sought to know Christ's intentions
      3. Christ knew what he had in mind and answered before the question was asked
   B. Nicodemus' question
      1. "How can such a thing be?" especially in my case
      2. Christ explains the meaning of "born-again"
         a. He speaks of water (repentance, washing) and the spirit (renewal)
         b. It is spelled out in Titus 3:5 and pictured by baptism cf. Colossians 2:12
         c. There is too little current emphasis on this
      3. Note the spiritual nature of the new birth
         a. Only that which is born of spirit can be spiritual (6)
         b. The new birth is invisible (8). (It is like the wind— seen only by its results and effects)

III. **The Correction in the Teaching (9-13)**
   A. An objection is raised
   B. The objectors are rebuked
      1. For failure to know the Scriptures (11)
      2. For not having received the witness that had been presented (12)
      3. For not understanding simple practical things (13)

IV. **The Detail of the Teaching (14-17)**
  A. A basic truth is involved here (14 & 15)
    1. An Old Testament picture is used (Numbers 21:6-9)
    2. The importance of belief is stressed (5 times in 4 verses)
  B. Its origin was in the plan of God (16)
    1. It is a gift of God because of the love of God
    2. The importance of faith is repeated
    3. Its freeness is stressed
  C. The purpose of the gift is given (17)
    1. Christ did not come primarily to judge
    2. Judgment comes because His first coming was not understood
    3. His primary purpose in coming was that the world might be saved through Him.

V. **The Application of the Teaching (18-21)**
  A. This makes a tremendous difference (18)
    1. There is no condemnation for the believer
    2. The unbeliever is under condemnation now
    3. This condemnation is caused by unbelief
  B. They show the reason that all don't believe (19)
    1. Men who refuse the light love darkness
    2. They do so because their deeds are evil
    3. The light is present to show up the situation
  C. They provide a way to tell if the difference has really been made
    1. Those who do evil want nothing or little to do with the light and the places where it is found.
    2. The ones who have the light want to be around the light

Conclusion:

Nicodemus came as a seeker. Jesus showed him how to find what would really help him. The key to the passage is in verse 3:16. Can you repeat it with your name in it?

You Only Live Twice
John 3:1-21

Introduction:

No matter where we go, we run into "jargon." Christianity has its "jargon" also, which is not too meaningful to those outside our fellowship. One of the key words we use is "born again." It is confusing to an outsider, at least it was to a man named Nicodemus. As Christ explains the concept to him, we can learn its meaning.

I. **It Is a Spiritual, Rather Than a Physical, Matter**
   A. "Born again" has an element of "born from above" in it
   B. Nicodemus didn't understand "from above" so
      1. He asked about the physical (4)
      2. Christ's answer removes his thinking from the mere physical (6 & 7)
   C. The words of Christ provide an actual definition
      1. You must be born "from above"
      2. This term "new birth" is used because of its similarity to physical birth
   D. Christ speaks of the two means involved (5). They speak of repentance and renewal
   E. Christ finalizes the whole matter with a plain statement: (6)
      1. There are two births
      2. Those who only have the first birth are only flesh
      3. Only those who are born from above possess the spiritual nature

II. **It Works in an Unseen Realm But Produces Visible Fruit**
   A. The illustration of the wind
      1. You see the effects of the wind and know by them that it blows
      2. It is the same with salvation: you can't see it, but you can know that it is present by the effects it produces.
   B. Notice this unseen aspect
      1. Salvation is in the realm of the subjective and intangible
         a. It is impossible to draw or package it
         b. It is no less real
      2. It is an area not readily lending itself to investigation
         a. It is very hard to be sure about another, neither yes nor no
         b. This should cause withheld judgment
   C. Notice the visible aspect
      1. We don't see the new birth, but we do see what it does in the lives of people.
      2. It will produce specific changes visible in the life

III. **It Is Absolutely Necessary**
   A. Notice the point-blank statements
      1. "Except a man be born again, he cannot see the kingdom of God"
      2. "Except a man be born of water and the spirit, he cannot enter into the kingdom"
   B. Why is it that one must be born again?
      1. Don't forget to whom Christ spoke these words
      2. "That which is born of the flesh is flesh"
   C. The urgency of the new birth
      1. Access to the kingdom depends on it
      2. The availability of the opportunity; it is for the present moment

IV. **It Is Secured in a Spiritual Manner**
   A. This is a physical impossibility
   B. The method that works
      1. Believe on the Lord Jesus Christ
      2. Repentance is necessary—no man truly turns to Christ who does not first know a desire to turn from himself and his sin
      3. The presence of the Spirit is necessary as He is the One who brings renewal
   C. Why the method works
      1. When Christ comes into the heart, the Spirit comes to dwell and can make the man whole and new
      2. The new dimension in life is introduced

Conclusion:
   That which is natural born is natural. It is born, lives, and dies. That which is spiritually born is spiritual. It is born, it lives, and it doesn't die.

When Life Begins
John 3:16

Introduction:

John 3:16 is a very favorite verse of many. A common misconception arises out of it. We need to identify and correct this.

I. **Common Misconceptions**
   A. The neutrality of the state of man
      1. Theology teaches that all are depraved
      2. In practice this is forgotten because all men don't act as bad as they could
   B. The idea of postponed punishment
      1. It is put in the future tense "you will"
      2. The idea is communicated that some day
         a. Believers shall be saved
         b. Unbelievers shall be lost

II. **Needful Correctives**
   A. Man is not neutral
      1. Romans 3:23 shows that all are born in sin
      2. Man is already condemned (John 3:17)
   B. Man's eternal state is begun now
      1. Perishing and eternal life are culminations of a process
      2. Proof: John 3:36, John 3:18, 1 Corinthians 1:18

III. **Obvious Implications**
   A. This points up our need to win the lost
      1. They are perishing right now
      2. They are living at far less than privilege
   B. It points up the need of urgency by the unconverted
      1. This is just not something limited to the future
      2. The soul now is in the process of dying
   C. This points up the difference that makes for change

IV. **Basic Encouragements**
   A. A reminder: We are now enjoying eternal life
      1. We need to remember this
      2. Eternal life is just an extension, in perfect form, of what we now have
   B. An exhortation: Let's live like it
      1. This is for our own benefit
      2. This is for the benefit of the lost

Conclusion:

Eternal life and eternal perishing are current issues, not future. If you know Christ, you already possess eternal life. If you do not know Him, you are already experiencing eternal perishing. Beware lest death overtake you suddenly and confirm eternal perishing.

The Greatest Verse in the Bible

John 3:16

Introduction:

Most people have a favorite verse or even a life verse. It will vary with individuals according to their situation and need. One favorite verse is full of "greatests." Count twelve of them with me.

I.   **The Greatest Lover—God**
   A. The ultimate reality
   B. The source of Love
      1. In Him and from Him
      2. He makes human love possible

II. **The Greatest Degree—So Loved**
   A. God loved the world
      1. He saw its situation
      2. He moved to meet that situation
   B. "So" speaks of degree
      1. He went beyond normal expectations
      2. He went to the furthest possible extent

III. **The Greatest Company—The World**
   A. This is a comprehensiveness beyond comprehension
      1. God loves all the world (those in the world)
      2. This includes all living and all who have ever lived
   B. No one is excluded

IV. **The Greatest Act—He Gave**
   A. God's action was giving
      1. This gift has no price tag
      2. Man has only to accept
   B. God did what was necessary

V.   **The Greatest Gift—His Only Begotten Son**
   A. Consider the gift, Christ
   B. God gave the most precious thing which could be given
      1. The One closest to Him
      2. The One who was part of Him

VI. **The Greatest Invitation—That Whosoever**
   A. It is absolutely open
   B. It is as expansive as the world
      1. It covers the same area
      2. It puts pressure on the individual

VII. **The Greatest Simplicity—Believeth**

A. A most basic truth
1. Christianity is the only religion requiring nothing but belief for heaven
2. There is no other condition
B. It becomes a stumbling block
1. Man has become conditioned to expect more
2. It appears too simple

VIII. The Greatest Attraction—In Him
A. Presents the object of belief
B. What an object He is

IX. The Greatest Promise—Should Not Perish
A. Relates to man's destiny
1. All are destined to hell
2. All look to eternal perishing
B. He provides the way of escape

X. The Greatest Difference—But
A. An interesting word in Scripture which always marks a clear contrast
B. In this particular case it marks the difference between heaven and hell

XI. The Greatest Certainty—Have
A. The word indicates complete possession, as belief makes possession absolutely sure
B. Note the present tense
1. Its means to have already
2. Eternal life begins now

XII. The Greatest Possession—Everlasting Life
A. It simply means what it says
1. It deals with life, real life
2. It deals with life which lasts forever
B. It contrasts with perishing

Conclusion:
This is the greatest verse in the Bible. You face the greatest decision in your life. Heaven and hell hang in the balance. Have you made the greatest choice?

I Am the Light of the World

John 8:12; 9:5

Introduction:

Blindness is actually perpetual darkness. By contrast we know how precious light really is. Jesus used light for one of His likenesses in John. He said, "I am the light of the world."

I. **A Revelation of Light (John 8:12; 9:5)**
   A. This is a favorite term with John (cf. John 1:1-10)
   B. Light defines darkness
      1. The two must go together for either to have meaning
      2. If He was light, then there must have been darkness in the world to which He came
   C. Light dispells darkness
      1. When light comes in, there is no more darkness
      2. The light He brought dispelled darkness everywhere

II. **A Reflection of Light (Matthew 5:14)**
   A. This seems contradictory, but John 9:5 explains it
      1. He is the light of the world; we are the light of the world
      2. A perfect analogy in nature: the sun and the moon
   B. This has a number of interesting implications
      1. This is a statement of fact—"ye are"
      2. This is a personal assignment
      3. We are totally dependent on Him to be any light at all

III. **A Rejection of Light (John 3:19-21)**
   A. Light has come
   B. Not everyone wanted the light
   C. The reason for not wanting light? Evil deeds
   D. Those who do not come to the light reveal that they do not want their deeds examined
   E. Those who come to the light reveal a desire for the truth

IV. **A Reception of Light (John 12:35 & 36)**
   A. Jesus speaks of accepting the light while there is time
   B. He urges men to become "children of light," those who are characterized by light, who walk in the light, who have accepted the light
   C. Notice how often darkness is connected with eternal damnation (2 Peter 2:4,17; Jude 6,13; Revelation 16:10)
   D. A conscious decision must be made regarding light. We are born in darkness and we must make a decision for light

Conclusion:

Jesus said, "I am the light of the world." Are you yet in darkness? Jesus said, "Ye are the light of the world."

I Am the Way

John 14:1-6

Introduction:

There is one good thing about a dark night: when the light shines through, it looks so much better. The disciples were going through a dark night. Christ gave them a ray of light.

I. **The Trigger**
   A. The context begins at chapter 13:1
      1. His message is now centering on bad themes: death, His departure, etc.
      2. The disciples were very upset by the end of chapter 13
   B. He comes with a message of comfort here: "Don't let your heart keep on being troubled"
      1. Keep on trusting in the Father and in Me (1)
      2. I have a reason for leaving, and it involves you (2)
      3. I will come again, and we will be together again (3)
      4. You already know how to follow me
   C. Thomas speaks for the group (15)
      1. "We don't know where you are going"
      2. "We don't know how to follow you"

II. **The Teaching**
   A. Personalizations
      1. "I am . . ." lays stress on Him as person
      2. He is obviously pointing to Himself
   B. Declarations—I am
      1. The life, 2. The truth, 3. The way
   C. Explanation
      1. Everything is perfected in God
      2. Christ is God
      3. He came and put us in touch with life, truth and provided the way

III. **The Test**
   A. Note the use of "the" which is a word of sole identification
   B. Note the clear statement, "no man cometh . . . but by me"
   C. Note the Scriptural support (John 3:3; 1 Timothy 2:5)
   D. Note the meaning
      1. No thing will do—it is personal
      2. No one else will do—"Me"

Conclusion:

We can expect to find life in Him, at least all life that is worth living. We can expect to find truth in Him, at least all truth that is ultimately measured by God's truth. We can expect to find the way to God in Him. Are you trying to come to Him by some other way?

Peter Preaches Christ

Acts 2:22-24

Introduction:

This is part of the first Christian sermon ever preached. Peter's understanding was awesome. Pentecost had taken place and raised all kinds of questions. Having answered their basic question, "What is this?," Peter launches into a discussion of Christ. We have before us Peter's fivefold identification of Christ:

I. **The Christ of the Natural—"Jesus of Nazareth" (22)**
    A. A common designation
        1. It distinguished Him from others of the same name
        2. It had a measure of opprobrium in it
    B. He started out where they were
        1. Everyone knew Him as the man from Nazareth
        2. Peter puts Him on the stage in this manner

II. **The Christ of the Supernatural—"Approved of God" (22)**
    A. It was "honorable"
        1. Approved by God "among you," means it was done in the midst of you
        2. "Ye yourself also know"
    B. It was "miraculous"
        1. Proved by His miracles
        2. Demonstrated by signs and wonders

III. **The Christ of Divine Direction—"Him Being Delivered" (23)**
    A. God had a special purpose for Him
        1. He was delivered by God
        2. This shows that God was not surprised and His sovereignty was not assailed
    B. Christ was in full accord with this purpose
        1. The word "counsel" involves discussion
        2. Christ was totally submissive to God's will
        3. He laid down His life; it was not actually taken from Him

IV. **The Christ of the Cross—"Crucified and Slain" (23)**
    A. Note the personal responsibility
        1. "Ye have taken," speaking to Jews
        2. "By the hands of the wicked," referring to the Romans
    B. A pernicious action
        1. Crucified. Refers to specific kind of death
        2. And slain. Even though He gave up His life, they had created the situation in which it occurred

V. **The Christ of the Resurrection—"Whom God Has Raised Up" (24)**
   A. The fact of the resurrection
   B. The necessity of the resurrection was that death could not hold Him

Conclusion:

This man Jesus was clearly approved by God. This man Jesus was willingly used by God to carry out His purposes. This man Jesus was crucified. This man Jesus was raised again by God's power. This is no mere man; this is the Divine Son of God!

Conversion

Acts 9:1-8

Introduction:

There are van conversions that make a plain van into a palace on wheels. That process is really a fairly good illustration of the biblical term, conversion.

I. **The Essence of Conversion**
   A. To turn
      1. From one way or thing *to* another (Luke 22:32; James 5:19 & 20)
      2. From one thing *into* another
   B. This is the manward side of the salvation transaction
   C. This is a momentary action rather than a process

II. **The Extent of Conversion**
   A. It is similar to a van conversion
      1. The exterior remains essentially the same
      2. The interior is changed
   B. Biblical teaching (1 Thessalonians 1:9; 2 Corinthians 5:17)
   C. When a man is converted, some things happen
      1. An internal change takes place, and it produces external signs
      2. This explains what happens to "good" people who get saved

III. **The Examples of Conversion**
   A. Peter—turned in salvation
      1. From self to Christ
      2. From weakness to strength
   B. Paul—turned in salvation
      1. From one morality to another
      2. What changed?
         a. Anger, pride, hatred
         b. Saw them as virtues; came to detest them as vices

IV. **The Essentiality of Conversion (Acts 26:17 & 18)**
   A. There is no conversion without some turning
      1. From one direction to another
      2. From one dominating principle to another
      3. From one determination to another
   B. The implications
      1. Salvation is more than praying a prayer
      2. Conversion involves turning
      3. If there is no turn, then there is no conversion!

Conclusion:

Have you been converted? What is causing you problems? God wants to change you inwardly.

What Is a Christian?

Acts 11:19-26

Introduction:

"What is a man?" He is so old, so tall, weighs so much, and has various features. That actually tells nothing about what the man really is; it just tell us what he looks like. So it is with Christianity. "What is a Christian?" He is someone who goes to church a lot, doesn't swear, doesn't smoke, doesn't gamble, etc. All those things also only tell us what he looks like. There is something far more central. Let's take a look at what a Christian really is:

I. **He Is a Person Who Believes in God**
   A. He does not believe in a God who is some great, external, world force
      1. The God that most people believe and the God that Christians believe are almost totally unrelated
      2. There are as many different "gods" as there are people who believe in God
   B. He does not believe in a God who is a figment of his own imagination or a creation of his own intellect
      1. He never says, "Now the way I see it is . . ."
      2. He does not try to create a God, "after his own image and likeness"
   C. He does believe in the God of the Bible
      1. His God is very precise and clearly defined
      2. He believes what He is told about God rather than believing what he thinks about God

II. **He Is a Person Very Conscious of Sin**
   A. He fully understands what sin really is
   B. He knows that he is a sinner by nature, and he knows that he commits sinful acts
   C. He knows that his sin is great
      1. There is nothing in himself adequate to please God
      2. It has separated him from God because of God's holiness
      3. It had to be dealt with by God because it is an issue too big for man to deal with unaided

III. **He Is a Person Willing to Do Things God's Way**
   A. He knows that God declared what is necessary for him to go to heaven: "Except a man be born again, he cannot see the kingdom of God"
   B. He knows that he must do it God's way for it to work out, and thus he doesn't try to do it his way.

C. He has found what God has said about how it must be done, and he has done it that way

IV. He Is a Person Who Has Made a Specific Decision at a Point in Time
A. He believes all the right things
    1. There is a God
    2. He is a sinner
    3. God is displeased with sin, and the sinner thus must die
    4. Christ was the Son of God
    5. Christ died for the sins of mankind so that mankind would not have to die for his own
B. He knows that all this has a personal application to him
C. He is one who has accepted personally what God has provided, required, and done

Conclusion:
The term is used loosely today, but that use is not accurate. In a biblical sense, it is reserved for those who have confessed their sin to God, asked His forgivness, and then asked Jesus Christ to be their personal Savior. Are you a Christian?

The Bare Essentials

Acts 16:30

Introduction:

The Philippian jailer put it into a simple form when he asked, "What must I do to be saved?" What is the minumum necessary to be saved? What are the bare essentials you must believe in order to come to saving knowledge of Christ? There are just five things essential. Many other things can wait until after salvation to be straightened out.

I. **You Are a Sinner**
   A. It is not hard to come to a clear definition of sin
      1. Sin is doing what is wrong
      2. Sin is failing to do what is right
   B. Most people are willing to admit that they are sinners
      1. Most disclaimers have to do with heinous sin
      2. Few would lay claim to perfection

II. **You Are a Lost Sinner**
   A. Many who will admit that they are sinners will not admit that they are lost
      1. "I do the best that I can," is most common
      2. Most people have some idea that good works are sufficient
   B. There can be no salvation until there is a recognition of one's need
      1. As a sinner there is *nothing* one can do to save himself
      2. One of the spiritual marks of sinfulness is helplessness

III. **Only God Can Help You**
   A. As a lost sinner, you cannot please God in any way
      1. "All our righteousnesses are as filthy rags" (Isaiah 64:6)
      2. There is no way you can get from where you are to where God is on your own
   B. You must be helped by God

IV. **God Has Already Helped You**
   A. God has already done what needed to be done for your salvation
      1. Christ has come and paid the price that needed to be paid
      2. God has already been satisfied
   B. There is nothing more that needs to be done
      1. The job is finished, every requirement has been met, every aspect fulfilled
      2. When we have done all, there is usually more to be done. That is not so here. It is all done

V. **You Must Receive His Help**
   A. You must stop depending on yourself
      1. Many want to "do" something
      2. Anything you do is self-dependent
   B. You must accept what Christ has done for you
      1. His work is of no avail if it is not accepted
      2. Acceptance is the only thing you can "do"

Conclusion:

What must I do to be saved? The next verse answers it, "Believe on the Lord Jesus Christ and thou shalt be saved." There is nothing else necessary. There is nothing else that will avail. There is nothing else that can be done. Have you done what needs to be done? Just trust Him as Savior.

Just As If

Romans 5:1-11

Introduction:

We often tell children that justified means "just as if I'd never sinned." This is not a very theological definition, but it is actually really accurate.

I. **Its Definition**
   A. Imagine a courtroom scene
      1. The prosecutor reads the charges
      2. A man admits his guilt
      3. A sentence is required ("soul that sinneth")
   B. He is more than declared "not guilty"
      1. All failure and sin are forgiven
      2. The person is viewed as if he had kept the law
      3. Additional privileges are granted

II. **Its Method**
   A. Sin and failure are not just glossed over
   B. Christ took care of both
      1. He paid the penalty for our sins
      2. He fulfilled the law for righteousness (Romans 10:4)

III. **Its Application**
   A. How does what He did get credited to our account?
      1. By our accepting Him
      2. When we accept Christ, we accept what He did as well
   B. This explains justification by grace through faith (God does it by grace, and it is applied by faith)

IV. **Its Benefits**
   A. It gives us standing with God
   B. It opens the box of His blessings (Romans 5:1-11)
   C. Judgment is thus moved up and completed (case can't be reopened)
   D. It grants status that can't be lost

Conclusion:

This is a big Bible theme—"Just as if I'd never sinned." The whole transaction is too big to be repeated. There is only one way to get to that place. We can only draw on what Christ has done. That is done through faith. Are you justified?

What More Do You Need?

Romans 5:8

Introduction:

The question of being under conviction is very significant. Many people are waiting for something special to happen before they make spiritual decisions. It is highly unlikely that something special will happen, however, because it already has.

I. **A Sorry State**
   A. The absence of conviction
      1. "I have never been convicted"
      2. Somehow that statement is used to remove the idea of responsibility
         a. I don't have to do something if I am not convicted
         b. I can only get saved if I am convicted of my need
   B. The operation of conviction
      1. Conviction is not something mystical
      2. Conviction is in conjunction with the truth
         a. The truth is found in the Word
         b. The Holy Spirit takes the Word and applies it
         c. The heart must then respond to the truth

II. **A Perfect Provision ("God commendeth His love . . .")**
   A. God's action
      1. God has already commended His love toward us
      2. Note that it is His own love
      3. It has already been commended (God has already provided what we need to be convicted)
   B. God's demonstration
      1. Christ has already died for us—nothing more is necessary
      2. This happened while we were yet sinners
      3. What is necessary for conviction has already happened

III. **A Required Response**
   A. Man must face the issue
      1. Man must think through what has already happened
         a. He is a sinner
         b. He is thus separated from God
         c. Christ has done what needs to be done
      2. Man must understand
         a. He must understand the true nature of conviction
         b. He must stop waiting for some light to dawn
      3. Man must accept the fact that God has already done what needs to be done

B. The fault lies with man
1. It lies with anyone who says, "I am not convicted about my need for salvation"
2. The facts are these
   a. God has already done everything He is ever going to do for your sin
   b. The Holy Spirit has recorded that fact in the Bible
   c. It is being preached
   d. The Holy Spirit is helping to apply it
   e. You must respond to the truth

Conclusion:

Anyone who is waiting for something to happen to convince him that he needs to be saved is in for a disappointment. All that is necessary for salvation has already been done. Respond to what God has already done and the Holy Spirit has already told you.

The Christian and Yom Kippur
Romans 5:10 & 11

Introduction:

Yom Kippur, the day of atonement, is a special day to the Jews. Considering the fact that the word atonement is used only once in the New Testament and not much more in the Old Testament, it is a very important concept. The concept is referred to at least 3,000 times. Actually it is a word created to describe a biblical truth. Atonement: at-one-ment.

I. **The Problem of Man**
   A. Man has a *big* problem, and the Bible makes it look *very bad* with the pictures it draws
      1. A slave needing to be bought back (Romans 7:14)
      2. An enemy needing placation (Colossians 1:21)
      3. A corpse needing resurrection (Ephesians 2:1, 5)
      4. A captive needing freedom (2 Timothy 2:26)
      5. A criminal needing pardon (Romans 7:22-25)
   B. It is difficult to make man's situation worse than it actually is

II. **The Provision of God**
   A. "Atonement" used once in New Testament
      1. Romans 5:10 & 11
      2. The Greek word is used four other times
      3. It is translated "reconcile"
   B. Reconciliation described (1 Corinthians 7:11)
      1. To make peace between, bring back together
      2. It assumes that God and man are estranged, but God does something about it

III. **The Prodecure of God**
   A. "Atonement" in Old Testament means "covering"
      1. It is the same word translated "mercy seat"
      2. Exodus 25:17-22
   B. Atonement is actually "covering"
      1. Leviticus 6
      2. The blood of an animal "covered" the sin of the people
   C. The covering was only temporary until the time of Christ
      1. Animal blood "covered"
      2. His blood "washed away" (1 John 1:7)

Conclusion:

Man was estranged from God. God made provision for reconciliation. Reconciliation is through the blood (death) of Christ. The only way to be "covered" is to accept Him. This is the reason why nothing we do can earn our way to God. We are too far off to get back on our own.

The Meaning of Salvation

Romans 10:9-13

Introduction:

Many don't know what salvation really means. A dictionary doesn't help much as it gives three meanings: to avoid expenditure, to put away for the future, and to keep from some harm or danger. The last is the basic biblical meaning.

I. **Salvation Has Two Aspects**
   A. It is *from* (Romans 5:9)
      1. Sin which results in
      2. Eternal death which results in
      3. Eternity in hell which is
      4. Under the power of Satan
   B. It is *to* (Hebrews 7:25)
      1. A term of duration
      2. To such things as
         a. Newness of life
         b. Freedom from sin
         c. Eternal life
         d. Joys of heaven

II. **Salvation Has Three Tenses**
   A. Past (2 Timothy 1:9) "have been saved"
      1. Refers to the finished work of Christ
      2. In this sense it is all over
   B. Present (1 Corinthians 1:18) "we are being saved"
      1. Refers to continuing work of Christ
      2. There is a sense in which it is presently going on
   C. Future (Romans 5:9 & 10) "we shall be saved"
      1. Refers to future work of Christ
      2. This is our anticipation
   D. The combination means that
      1. We have been saved from sin's penalty
      2. We are being saved from sin's power
      3. We will be saved from sin's presence

III. **Salvation Has One Means**
   A. This is abundantly clear (Acts 4:12), but nothing is challenged more than this
      1. "None other name"
      2. "Under heaven"
      3. "Given among men"
      4. "Whereby we *must*"
      5. "Be saved"

B. It is illustrated in Acts 16
C. It is explained in Romans 10

Conclusion:

We are not fooling with something trivial. These are matters of sin, life and death, and eternity. God knows best about how we can get to Himself. "Saved" is the most important word of all. Is it a personal word to you?

This New Life of Yours

1 Corinthians 6:19-20

Introduction:

One of the reasons Paul used to show why going to law against other believers was wrong was the fact that unbelievers are the kinds of people that believers once were. In the process of showing this, he presents a fantastic argument and some spectacular teaching that answers our questions and challenges our living.

I. **The Past**
   A. "Such were some of you"
      1. Notice first the tense here—*were*
      2. Some of you—no one was all of these, and some likely were none of them
   B. Note the following:
      1. "Effeminate" refers to male prostitutes or to transvestites
      2. "Abusers of themselves with mankind" refers to homosexuals
   C. These actions represent the kinds of things which characterize people who are not headed for heaven

II. **The Present**
   A. The things that have happened
      1. "You are washed"—this means that the guilt has been cared for
      2. "You are justified"—this means to be made just-as-if-you had not sinned, and it means you have the righteousness of Christ
      3. "You are sanctified"—this means that you have the potential for holiness imparted
   B. The people they have happened to
      1. These things are all done in the realm where the Lord Jesus works
      2. They are all possible by the power of the Holy Spirit working within your hearts

III. **The Practicalities**
   A. God can and does save anyone
      1. This is all He had to work with in Corinth
      2. No matter what a person has done, he can be saved by the power of God
   B. Salvation means an end to wrong conduct
      1. The past tense is incredibly important
      2. Old things can no longer dominate our lives

C. Salvation and attendant forgiveness are complete
   1. The "were" indicates that all is changed
   2. Their presence in the church and the way in which he talks of the church makes full forgiveness completely obvious
D. Change is possible
   1. Even things we hold can't be changed are changeable, such as alcoholism and homosexuality
   2. God has done what we need done to effect change. Failure to know change is not a matter of God failing to do for us, nor even of our own inability. It is a matter of failing to take hold of what God has already done for us
E. The new things we have in Christ make change absolutely necessary

Conclusion:

What are you doing about the dominating sin in your life? God has made the provision; you need to use it. Continuing in sin is wrong when freedom and victory are available.

What's New

2 Corinthians 5:17

Introduction:

People sometimes tell Christians, "You don't know what you're missing." The truth is, "You don't know what you've got." Those who "have it" don't always know what they've got, and those who don't "have it," don't know what they are missing.

I. **What Does It Mean to Be "in Christ"?**
   A. This is primarily a matter of relationship
      1. We trust in Him
      2. We live in Him
      3. We are related to Him
   B. Every person who has genuinely accepted Christ as his personal Savior is "in Him."

II. **What Does Being "in Christ" Mean to Us?**
   A. Security (John 10:27-29)
      1. Our relationship is not a revolving door
      2. He has already borne God's judgment on sin and further judgment of us would be unjust
   B. Acceptance with God (Ephesians 1:6)
      1. God said, "In Him I am well pleased," of only one person
      2. If we are in Him, we have the same said of us. God sees Him when He looks at us
   C. Assurance for the future (John 14:19)
      1. He is the resurrection and the life
      2. In Him we have both resurrection and life
   D. An inheritance in glory (Romans 8:14-17)
      1. As the only begotten Son, He is God's sole heir
      2. We are His heirs, so we share in the inheritance
   E. Participation in the divine nature (2 Peter 1:4)
      1. As divine He has a divine nature
      2. If we are "in Him," we share in that nature
   F. Knowledge (John 16:13-15)
      1. He is defined as truth (John 1:14, 14:6)
      2. In Him we share a nature defined as truth

III. **How Does One Get to Be "in Christ"?**
   A. Those who receive Him become His children, and are in Him
   B. We get to be in Him by trusting Him as Savior

Conclusion:

Those "in Him" often don't know what they have. They fail to accept all it provides and live in lack of assurance and fear of loss. They also act like it doesn't matter how they live. Those out of Him don't know what they miss. There is so much there for you.

Resurrection Realities

2 Corinthians 5:17

Introduction:

Easter commemorates one of the great changes of history, from a broken, battered body and death, despair, defeat, and despondency to a renewed body, victory, and excitement. Such change is an essential issue in Christianity.

I. **The Cruciality of Change**
   A. Salvation includes change
      1. It is called the new birth
      2. It is called a quickening
      3. It is called a new creation
   B. Something so radical can hardly be without its effects
      1. It produces a change of attitude
      2. It produces a change of feeling
      3. It produces a change of character
   C. Genuine salvation will produce some type of change
      1. It may be embryonic
      2. It may be primarily internal
      3. It may take time to develop

II. **The Characteristics of Change**
   A. Change is an exciting possibility
      1. It deals effectively with the past
      2. It means the possibility of freedom
      3. It opens doors to tomorrow
   B. Change is a guided process
      1. It doesn't place us at the mercy of the unknown
      2. It is according to a plan
      3. It brings us back into accord with God's original plan for our lives
   C. Change is of varying degree
      1. There will be at least some change
      2. It all depends on the point of beginning
      3. It depends on our willingness to have it

III. **The Challenge of Change**
   A. Spiritual change comes from within
      1. God's change is "inside-out"
      2. It distinguishes between real and apparent change
      3. It makes external change more possible
   B. There should be change
      1. If one is saved, there is change

    2. There should be much change
    3. We ought to be cultivating change
  C. You can know change
    1. It comes from being in Christ
    2. It involves trusting Him as Savior
    3. It is open to any man

Conclusion:

God wants to change you into what He wants you to be (which is very clear from the Bible). Will you know change?

Any Other Gospel

Galatians 1:6-10

Introduction:

We live in an age of experts, which wouldn't be so bad were it not for the fact that everyone considers himself an expert. This is especially true in the field of religion, where everyone seems to have an opinion of how things ought to be. We need to go back and find out what the Bible has to say on the subject—at least on the subject of salvation. Missing the truth in this area could be fatal

I. **Basic Approaches (There are 4 Gospels being proclaimed today)**
   A. The Gospel of indifference
      1. It various forms
         a. "I really don't care"
         b. "It will take care of itself"
         c. "I'm not interested"
      2. Behind it all lies a philosophy which holds that if one ignores it, it will go away or take care of itself
   B. The Gospel of works
      1. The basic American religion
      2. This is typical of so many religious groups
   C. The Gospel of contemplation
      1. Salvation is part of a process of mind
      2. This involves the Eastern mystery religions
   D. The Gospel of Grace
      1. Salvation is something God has done for us when we deserved nothing but judgment
      2. In this Gospel there is nothing for man to do but believe

II. **Basic Arguments (there are two basic arguments)**
   A. There are many ways to heaven
      1. All ways lead to heaven
      2. What you believe is not important. What is important is that you do believe or how you believe (salvation by sincerity)
   B. There is only way to heaven
      1. This is what the Bible teaches: John 3:3; 1 Timothy 2:15; John 14:6
      2. This is in accord with logic
      3. This is in accord with personal experience

III. **Basic Assertions (Paul believed in the idea of one way so firmly that he made strong statements about other Gospels)**
   A. Other Gospels are alien

1. The Gospel is fixed
2. There really is no other Gospel at all (7a)

B. Other Gospels are alluring
1. They are very subtle (they seem angelic)
2. Even preachers can change
    a. It is not what a man preaches but what the Bible teaches
    b. There is an open invitation to check it out

C. Other Gospels are anathema
1. The penalty of preaching another Gospel is to be accursed in the sight of God
2. The penalty is severe because such teaching leads men to hell

IV. Basic Applications

A. Which Gospel are you following?
1. Indifference
2. Works
3. Contemplation
4. Grace

B. Will it get you where you want to go?
1. You say, "I'll take my chances"
2. Wouldn't it be wise to improve those chances?

C. Why not accept the Gospel?
1. It may seem too simple
2. It is what the Bible teaches

Conclusions:

Are you an expert on religion? Be careful of such expertise as it may keep you out of heaven and send you to hell.

How to Be a Spiritual Christian: Spiritual Growth

Ephesians 4:14-16

Introduction:

There is nothing more tragic than a baby who doesn't grow. It causes crushed dreams, trampled hopes, and heartbreaking realities. God faces this every day. Are you one whose lack of growth grieves the Father? The Bible makes a strong case for spiritual growth

I.   The Means of Growth—"Truth"
    A.   This is the key to any and all growth
    B.   This is truth in the spiritual realm
        1.   It must be based upon the Bible
        2.   There is such a thing as truth

II.   The Mark of Growth—"Love"
    A.   Love for God
        1.   This must be more than lip service
        2.   This is practical devotion
    B.   Love for the Word
        1.   This demands practical demonstration
        2.   This requires positive obedience
    C.   Love for the saints
        1.   This involves continued fellowship
        2.   This results in community feeling

III.   The Measure of Growth—"Christ"
    A.   Likeness to Christ is the issue
    B.   Growth leads to maturity

IV.   The Magnitude of Growth—"In All Things"
    A.   Every area of life is involved
        1.   There is a difference between the secular and the sacred
        2.   The inward and the outward are alike
    B.   This is especially true in our weak spots
        1.   They allow us the largest room for growth
        2.   They show the greatest need

V.   The Manner of Growth—"From Him"
    A.   He is our source
        1.   Everything comes from Him
        2.   This is especially true of growth
    B.   We must make an effort and stay open to His working
        1.   We must use the means at our disposal
        2.   We must exert effort
    C.   He gives the growth

VI. The Method of Growth—"The Edifying of Itself"

A. This refers to the integration of the body
   1. This is a cycle
   2. The essential nature of the body is self-integration
B. This refers to the function of each member
   1. There should be no missing parts
   2. Personal problems should not be allowed to affect the whole
C. This refers to the fulfillment of function
   1. Sometimes the church is "the hobbled household"
   2. We must help the injured individual

Conclusion:

If you are not closer to the Lord than you were six months ago, you are not growing. If you are not growing, you are not pleasing Christ. If you are not growing, you do not show the evidence of spirituality. Growth involves commitment, determination, application, and desire. Are you a growing Christian?

That Glorious Gospel

Colossians 1:5

Introduction:

Everyone talks about the Gospel. We have Gospel preaching, teaching and singing. We share the Gospel, believe the Gospel, and proclaim the Gospel. But it is not always obvious that everyone understands the Gospel they promote.

I. **The Gospel Is the Truth ("... the truth of the Gospel")**
   A. It is absolute truth with no error in it
   B. It is ultimate truth; the greatest truth that there can possibly be
   C. It is supreme truth; no truth can mean more to us

II. **The Gospel Is Communicated ("the Word ... of the Gospel")**
   A. It was lived in the person of Christ
   B. It was written on the pages of the Bible
   C. It is spoken by men in order to be made meaningful

III. **The Gospel Is Revealed ("which is come unto you as it is in all the world ...")**
   A. It has come into the world
   B. It has come into all the world
   C. It has come to you and me

IV. **The Gospel Is Theological**
   A. It involves the grace of God (favor where punishment is well-deserved). The Gospel is good news where bad news is expected and proper
   B. It involves being made meet for the "inheritance of the saints in light" (12b)
      1. An "inheritance" comes by gift and is not earned
      2. "Of saints," those belonging to a particular group
      3. "In light," the place of God's dwelling in contrast to Satanic operation
      4. "Partakers," those who share in it
      5. "Meet," suited or prepared, qualified for
      6. God has created this situation. It is not something done for oneself
   C. It involves deliverance
      1. He has rescued us from the dominion of darkness
      2. He has lifted us out of what we had by nature
   D. It involves translation
      1. He has not just "taken us out"

       2. He has relocated us, made us part of the kingdom of light ruled by His Son
- E. It involves redemption
  1. It means to be bought back for a price
  2. The price was His death
- F. It involves forgiveness
  1. We have not been brought out with a guilty conscience
  2. He has dealt with all guilt, judicial, moral, and psychological

V. The Gospel Results in Fruitbearing
- A. It produces the fruit of our lips which is praise
- B. It produces the fruit of the Spirit developed progressively in our lives
- C. It produces the fruit of good works, things specifically done in the name of the Lord Jesus
- D. It produces the fruit of souls saved. Why should it stop with you and me?

Conclusion:

The Gospel is truth conceived in God. It has been revealed to mankind: it has been communicated to individuals; it is filled with thrilling facts; and it is designed to bring forth fruit. Have you accepted it? Do you understand what it involves? Are you bringing forth fruit as a result of it?

What Was, What Is, and Why

Colossians 1:20-23

Introduction:

The Savior is superior in many ways. The greatest superiority of all lies in what He has done for sinners. This refers to you and me, and it is helpful to review it periodically.

I. **What Was (v. 21)**
    A. We started out alienated and estranged
        1. We belonged to someone else, although we were not aware of it
        2. We have been transferred to another owner
    B. We started out enemies in mind with hostile dispositions
        1. Our hostility was directed to God
        2. It was a matter of choice and our own fault
    C. We were dominated by wicked works and evil deeds (3:5-9)
        1. This was evil behavior
        2. It arose out of hostility

II. **What Is (v. 22b)**
    A. We are now holy
        1. We are cleansed from sin
        2. We are separated unto God and His service
    B. We are now unblameable
        1. We are without any blemish at all
        2. We are worthy of being offered to God
        3. We are faultless in His sight
    C. We are now unreproveable
        1. We are without legal charge against us
        2. We are completely above reproach or attack

III. **How It Happened (v. 20, 22a)**
    A. God reconciled all things to Himself
        1. To "reconcile" means "to change so as to bring into accord with"
        2. God did it, so we are reconciled to Him, and not the reverse
        3. He reconciled all things in earth or heaven, everything reconcileable
    B. God did it through the death of Christ
        1. "Having made peace"
        2. "Through His blood"
        3. "In the body of His flesh"

IV. What It All Means (v. 23)

   A. Hold what you believe
      1. "If ye continue in the faith"—assuming you continue in the faith
      2. There is no room for loss of faith as continuing shows genuineness
   B. Be what you are
      1. You are grounded and settled
      2. This means to be in practice what you are in position
   C. Proclaim what you know
      1. The Word of the truth of the Gospel is involved
      2. You are responsible to share what has happened to you with others

Conclusion:

Paul's strong teaching brings out three important truths: 1). Hold to what you believe 2.) Be what you really are 3). Proclaim what you know by personal experience. By doing so, you can show the superiority of the Savior in a practical way.

Regeneration
Titus 3:5

Introduction:

There is a difference between complex and complicated. Complex means to be made up of many parts, intricate. Complicated means confusing, hard to understand or explain. Salvation is very complex. It involves many parts: repentance, faith, justification, sanctification, conversion and regeneration. But it is utterly uncomplicated. Regeneration is part of this complex transaction.

I. **Its Meaning**
   A. Inner renewal (recreation of fallen man by the Spirit of God at the time a man becomes a Christian)
   B. The change God effects in us when we accept Christ
   C. We turn (conversion) as a result of a change of mind (repentance), and then He changes us (regeneration)

II. **Its Manner**
   A. It is instantaneous
       1. When the Spirit comes
       2. The Spirit comes at the moment of salvation
   B. It is spiritual
       1. It is internal
       2. It is invisible
   C. It is influential
       1. It causes outward signs
       2. It becomes visible through effects
   D. It is unexplainable
       1. We have no idea of how the Holy Spirit does it
       2. This takes nothing away from the truth
   E. It is potential
       1. The resulting change is not automatic
       2. The potential for change is present

III. **Its Implications**
   A. A Gospel chorus expresses it perfectly - "Things are different now"
   B. This is the difference between "profession" and "possession"
   C. It affects outward results

Conclusion:

If there is no change whatever, then there is probably no new birth. Some have the problem of failure to live up to their potential. We need to ask, "Am I regenerate?" If so, why doesn't it show more?

Growth in Grace
2 Peter 3:18

Introduction:

This is one of the dominant themes of the Bible, although it is not often expressed in so many words. It is also one of the dominant themes of the Bible and of all Christianity.

I. **That in Which We Are to Grow—Grace**
   A. We are to grow in the knowledge of Christ
      1. This includes what we *know about* Christ
      2. This includes what we *experience* of Christ
   B. We are to grow in grace
      1. This involves everything that God gives us
      2. Our faith is more than a set of beliefs, it is also a life-style

II. **How We Are to Grow**
   A. It is progressive
      1. Have you progressed further than you were a year ago?
      2. Have you progressed further than ever before?
   B. It is expanding
      1. Spiritual life should be ever bigger and broader
      2. Are you a better Christian than you have ever been?
   C. It is maturing
      1. Maturing is to be what one is designed to be
      2. Are you more than you were before?
   D. It is stabilizing
      1. The fuller the growth of the plant, the less likely it is that it will be uprooted
      2. Most of those who drift from Christianity have not grown
      3. The best guarantee against aberration is to grow the way one ought to grow
   E. It is fruit-bearing
      1. Most plants are designed to bear fruit or flower
      2. No fruit in life means no purpose fulfilled

III. **How We Start the Growth**
   A. Note that it says , "grow *in* grace"
      1. It does not say "grow *into* grace"
      2. It does not say that we have to keep being planted
   B. You must be in grace to grow in grace
      1. The only way to be in grace is the way God has provided
      2. You only get into His grace by trusting His Son
      3. If you are not born again, you are not in grace

Conclusion:

God's church only grows as people come to grace and as people grow in grace. Have you ever trusted Christ as your Savior? Are you growing in grace? Have you slipped back from where you once were?